D0583613

Taschek, Karen, 1956–
Daughters of liberty :
the American Revolution
c2011.
33305223725536
sa   05/08/12

Daughters of Liberty:
The American Revolution
and the Early Republic
1775–1827

KAREN TASCHEK

CHELSEA HOUSE
An Infobase Learning Company

DAUGHTERS OF LIBERTY: THE AMERICAN REVOLUTION AND THE EARLY REPUBLIC 1775–1827

Copyright © 2011 Bailey Publishing Associates Ltd

Produced for Chelsea House by Bailey Publishing Associates Ltd, 11a Woodlands, Hove BN3 6TJ, England

All rights reserved. No part of this book may be reproduced or utilized in any form or by any means, electronic or mechanical, including photocopying, recording, or by any information storage or retrieval systems, without permission in writing from the publisher. For information contact: Chelsea House, an imprint of Infobase Learning, 132 West 31st Street, New York, NY 10001

Library of Congress Cataloging-in-Publication Data
Taschek, Karen, 1956–
  Daughters of liberty: the American Revolution and the Early Republic, 1775–1827 / Karen Taschek.
    p. cm. — (A cultural history of women in America)
  Includes index.
  ISBN 978-1-60413-928-0
  1. Women—United States—Social conditions—18th century. 2. Women--United States—Social conditions—19th century. 3. Women—Political activity—United States—History—18th century. 4. Women—Political activity—United States--History—19th century. 5. United States—History—Revolution, 1775–1783—Women. I. Title.
  HQ1416.T37 2011
  305.40973'09033—dc22
                              2010033717

Chelsea House books are available at special discounts when purchased in bulk quantities for businesses, associations, institutions, or sales promotions. Please call our Special Sales Department in New York at (212) 967-8800 or (800) 322-8755.

You can find Chelsea House on the World Wide Web at: http://www.chelseahouse.com

Project management by Patience Coster
Text design by Jane Hawkins
Picture research by Shelley Noronha
Printed and bound in Malaysia
Bound book date: April 2011

10 9 8 7 6 5 4 3 2 1

This book is printed on acid-free paper.

All links and Web addresses were checked and verified to be correct at the time of publication. Because of the dynamic nature of the Web, some addresses and links may have changed since publication and may no longer be valid.

The publishers would like to thank the following for permission to reproduce their pictures:
The Art Archive: 5 (Culver Pictures), 7 (Private Collection/Marc Charmet), 8 (Culver Pictures), 18 (Superstock), 30 (Superstock), 32 (National Archives Washington DC), 37 (Culver Pictures), 38 (The Granger Collection); The Bridgeman Art Library: 26 (Massachusetts Historical Society), 29 (Massachusetts Historical Society), 31 (Victoria & Albert Museum, London), 33 (Museum of Fine Arts, Boston, Massachusetts, Bequest of Winslow Warren), 34 (Smithsonian Institution), 40 (Gift of Mrs William L. Little, 1979), 49 (Atwater Kent Museum of Philadelphia), 57 (Nativestock Pictures); Cataragui Archaeological Research Foundation: 17; Corbis: 14 (Bettmann), 19 (Bettmann), 28 (Francis G. Mayer), 42 (Geoffrey Clements), 44 (Philadelphia Museum of Art), 48 (Bettmann), 50 (The Gallery Collection), 54 (Bettmann); John Carter Brown Library: 24; The Library of Congress: 6, 9, 12, 15, 22 (The Gerlach-Barklow Col., Joliet, Ill., U.S.A, No. M2207), 27 (Library of Congress Rare Book & Special Collections Division); Mary Evans Picture Library: 25, 39 (Interfoto), 41, 58; Ronald Grant Archive: 23 (Columbia Pictures); Terra Foundation for American Art, Chicago: 53; TopFoto: 10 (The Granger Collection), 11 (The Granger Collection), 13 (The Granger Collection), 16 (The Granger Collection), 20 (The Granger Collection), 21 (The Granger Collection), 35 (The Granger Collection), 36 (The Granger Collection), 43 (The Granger Collection), 45 (The Granger Collection), 46 (The Granger Collection), 47 (The Granger Collection), 51 (The Image Works), 52 (The Granger Collection), 55 (The Granger Collection), 56 (The Granger Collection), 59 (The Granger Collection).

CONTENTS

THIS BOOK LOOKS AT THE PERIOD OF history in which the United States of America came into existence and broke away from Britain. It examines the lives of women during that time and their role in the Revolutionary War and its aftermath.

In the winter and early spring of 1775, the thirteen colonies that would become the first United States teetered on the brink of war with Britain. The colonies—New York, Massachusetts, Maryland, Delaware, New Jersey, Pennsylvania, Virginia, Rhode Island, New Hampshire, Connecticut, North Carolina, South Carolina, and Georgia— had for a long time protested unfair taxes, without representation. They also objected to being governed by Britain, where most of the Americans or their recent ancestors were from. Then on April 19, 1775, the Revolutionary War began with the battles of Lexington and Concord. After eight long years, the thirteen colonies won the war and were free to form a new country, the United States of America.

The war brought great changes in the mindset and activities of women. Before the war, women had mostly stayed home, doing housework and raising children. When the Revolution began, women became pivotal in the war effort. They boycotted British goods such as tea and cloth, replacing the imported goods with homespun and other substitutes. Some women went to war alongside men while others ran the farms and businesses at home, finding they could manage them efficiently and well. Women fought off roving armies and passionately debated the new political system. Against this dramatic backdrop, women formed political associations for the first time—among them the Daughters of Liberty.

66

THE WOMEN'S BOYCOTT

If the sons, so degenerate! the blessings despise,
Let the Daughters of Liberty nobly arise;
And though we've no voice but a negative here,
The use of the taxables, let us forbear:—
(Then merchants import till your stores are all full,
May the buyers be few, and your traffic be dull!)

An anonymous author described the Daughters of Liberty in a poem in the *Pennsylvania Gazette* in 1768.

Left: Lydia Darrah, an American Quaker, gives news of British troop movements to Lieutenant Colonel Thomas Craig, one of General George Washington's aides, near Philadelphia on December 3, 1777.

CHAPTER I
WOMEN OF THE ERA

IN THE 1770S, BEFORE THE AMERICAN REVOLUTION, women were expected to marry and raise a family. Most families lived on farms, so women pitched in and did whatever was needed to help their families survive. However, as the movement for revolution began, women joined together and used their purchasing power and practical skills to help in the fight for freedom.

C. January 1770

WILLIAM JACKSON,

an IMPORTER; at the

BRAZEN HEAD,

North Side of the TOWN-HOUSE,

and Opposite the Town-Pump, in

Corn-hill, BOSTON.

It is desired that the SONS and DAUGHTERS of LIBERTY, would not buy any one thing of him, for in so doing they will bring Disgrace upon themselves, and their Posterity, for ever and ever, AMEN.

Above: A Revolutionary paper from January 1770, before the war began, from the "Sons and Daughters of Liberty," announcing that they will boycott the goods of "William Jackson, an Importer."

A MAN'S WORLD

Once they were married, women stayed home, running the household day to day, bearing and looking after children, and nursing the sick. The man of the family voted in elections, served in the military, stood for public office, or ran a business. At home, the man handled the household money and oversaw the children's upbringing. This arrangement succeeded as long as the husband could work and stay alive. If her husband died, a wife would often know nothing of his debts or what the family property was worth.

WOMEN'S WORK

Farmwork before the age of agricultural machinery kept men and women busy. Few necessary items could be bought at the store. Women did spinning, weaving, sewing, washing, ironing, and baking on a regular basis. Some women's work on the farm was done every season. Mary Cooper of Oyster Bay, Long Island, wrote in her diary in 1769 that she did house cleaning in spring and the harvesting of cherries in midsummer. After a hog was butchered in winter, she used the tallow (fat) to make soap and candles. The men had less predictable tasks and sometimes went to town on business or hunted and fished. Children helped as best they could.

FRONTIER FOLK

On the frontier, women living in colonial America worked even harder and had few possessions. They often used gourds for cups and ate with their fingers. Native American women cultivated

Above: New York City as it looked in late-18th-century America.

crops while the men hunted and fished, and families wore animal skins and furs for clothes. Slave women did whatever was required of them, including work in the fields.

TOWNSWOMEN

Colonial women living in town might have fewer chores, depending on how rich they were. Cloth could be bought, so wealthier women didn't have to spin, but they often kept a garden or chickens for food. In those days, most women rose early—Abigail Adams, the wife of future president John Adams, got up at five every morning. City women's chores were similar to those of countrywomen: they did washing, ironing, and cooking and preserved fruit and vegetables.

However, unlike countrywomen, city women could buy most of their meat, vegetables, cheese, and butter at markets. Some of them used the time they saved doing this to clean their homes. Wives might also help their husband in the family store or business.

TURNING POINT

COURTSHIP CUSTOMS

Before the Revolutionary War, courting couples had to obey strict rules of modest behavior. Parents supervised these relationships and could approve of or end them. During the war years, many women were left alone as head of the household. These women's daughters, who had watched their independent mothers successfully deal with challenging situations, were much more likely to insist on choosing their own husbands.

Right: At the Boston Tea Party, colonists throw tea from ships into Boston Harbor to protest taxes. Women disguised the participants as Native Americans.

WOMEN'S CONTRIBUTION

"The ladies, while they vie with each other in skill and industry in their profitable employment, may vie with the men in contributing to the preservation and prosperity of their country and equally share in the honor of it. . . .

"The women might recover to this country the full and free enjoyment of all our rights, properties, and privileges (which is more than the men have been able to do) through their sacrifices and spinning."

From the *Boston Evening Post* newspaper, 1769

HOME LIFE

Wealthy women could afford to hire help in the form of servants, although they then needed to supervise them. Wealthy city women sometimes did lead the good life—rising late, taking music and dancing lessons, seeing friends, and reading the latest novel. Almost all women, in the city or country, rich or poor, learned to sew. They made shirts for the men and aprons, caps, and dresses for themselves. They also mended and altered clothes.

POLITICAL ASSOCIATIONS

The British wanted to raise money to pay for the defense and administration of their American colonies. On June 27, 1767, the British Parliament passed the Townsend Act (also known as the Revenue Act). This introduced taxes on tea, paper, paint, and many other British imports, causing an outcry among colonists. Immediately the colonists decided to boycott British manufactured goods, including tea and cloth. Although in colonial days Americans loved their tea (they were still British subjects), most of them vowed to do without it or to drink herbal teas, coffee, or other substitutes. To produce cloth, women across the country formed spinning groups, sometimes calling themselves the Daughters of Liberty. Men and women proudly began to wear homespun goods instead of manufactured, elegant clothes from Britain.

In a typical meeting of the Daughters of Liberty, as many as a hundred women might gather at the home of their church minister. Working at their spinning wheels, the women would talk about the issues of the day, eating only American foods and drinking herbal tea. Sometimes the women would compete to see who could spin the most and the best. At the end of the meeting, the ladies would give the spun yarn or thread to the minister.

Below: In *The Edenton Ladies' Tea Party*, a British cartoonist portrays the women who had signed the Edenton Resolution as wild partygoers.

A SOCIETY of PATRIOTIC LADIES.

TURNING POINT

THE EDENTON RESOLUTION

In October 1774, 51 women in Edenton, North Carolina, signed a resolution protesting taxes imposed by Britain. It stated: "As we cannot be indifferent on any occasion that appears nearly to affect the peace and happiness of our country, and as it has been thought necessary for the public good, to enter into several particular resolves by a meeting of members deputed from the whole Province, it is a duty which we owe." For many of the women who signed the petition, this was their first political act.

TURNING POINT

THE SONS OF LIBERTY

Much like the Daughters of Liberty, the Sons of Liberty, who formed in 1756, were committed to the cause of revolution in the colonies. At first, they only spread the word about British attacks on the colonists' freedom. But by 1765, in protest over the Stamp Act, which placed a levy on many imported items from Britain, the Sons of Liberty were committing illegal acts. These included burning in effigy or tarring and feathering unpopular people such as tax collectors in Boston and other cities.

CHAPTER 2

WOMEN AT WAR

FOLLOWING THE BATTLES OF LEXINGTON AND CONCORD in April 1775, the thirteen American colonies were at war with Britain. For the next eight years, battles ravaged the cities and the countryside. Women were involved in the Revolutionary War as camp followers, washing and cooking for the soldiers, and producing goods. Some acted as spies and delivered secret messages; others even fought in battles, disguised as men.

> ## *BREAKTHROUGH BIOGRAPHY*

MARTHA WASHINGTON (1731–1802)

Martha Washington was the wife of George Washington and the first lady of the new United States. During the Revolutionary War, she left the Washingtons' comfortable plantation, Mount Vernon in Virginia, to live with George wherever the headquarters of the Continental Army happened to be. In the winter of 1778–79, Martha joined the army camp at Valley Forge, Pennsylvania, where about 11,000 men were starving, freezing, and dressed in shredded clothing. Many of them were shoeless. Martha quickly organized women to sew shirts, knit stockings, and mend the men's clothes. Later, as first lady, Martha set a modest style for the first ladies who would come after her: she insisted on being addressed as "Mrs. Washington" rather than the grander title of "Lady Washington."

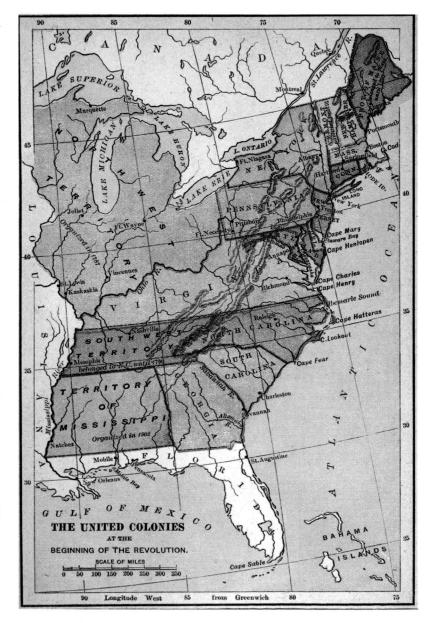

Right: This map shows the thirteen original colonies in about 1775. These colonies fought the Revolutionary War and formed the first government of the new United States.

THE WOMEN OF 76
TIDINGS FROM LEXINGTON.

Above: Seventeen-year-old patriot Sybil Ludington rallies the colonial militia on April 26, 1777.

♥ **WOMEN OF COURAGE AND CONVICTION**

DEBORAH SAMPSON (1760–1827)

Deborah Sampson grew up a servant after her father abandoned his family. Hard work in the house and fields made her strong. On May 20, 1782, at age twenty-one, Deborah enlisted in the Fourth Massachusetts Regiment of the Continental Army under the name Robert Shurtleff. Passing herself off as a man meant that other soldiers teased her because she did not need to shave, but she performed her duties as well as any man. Wounded in the leg during a battle at Tarrytown, New York, Deborah tended her own injury to avoid discovery as a woman, but she was found out while hospitalized with a fever and discharged from the military. The state of Massachusetts awarded her a pension for her service. After the war, wearing her military uniform, Deborah traveled around the country lecturing about her wartime experiences. Her children were awarded compensation as the heirs of "a soldier of the Revolution."

TAKING SIDES

Once the war had begun, colonial women were required to take sides in the conflict and declare themselves either loyalist, on the side of Britain, or patriot, on the side of American independence. Friendships between neighbors were lost and marriages broken up as people chose sides. But no matter which side women were on, soon they all found themselves trying to survive, as women's rights advocate Abigail Adams put it, "the terror of roving armies."

FOLLOWERS AND SOLDIERS

As camp followers, women accompanied the army of a husband or other family member. They were also involved in combat, taking the place of a wounded man or disguising themselves as men and joining the army as soldiers. Most women remained at home with children and property, but staying home did not guarantee staying out of the battles.

One of the worst aspects of the war was its duration—from spring 1775 until September 3, 1783. Because the men were involved in the fighting away from home, their wives were left alone as the head of the household. They had to feed and house

THE PENNSYLVANIA MAGAZINE: OR, AMERICAN MONTHLY MUSEUM. MDCCLXXV.

VOLUME I.

JUVAT IN SYLVIS HABITARE.

PHILADELPHIA:

PRINTED AND SOLD BY R. AITKEN, PRINTER AND BOOKSELLER, OPPOSITE THE LONDON COFFEE-HOUSE, FRONT-STREET.

LOVE OF PUBLIC GOOD

"Our ambition is kindled by the fame of those heroines of antiquity, who have rendered their sex illustrious, and have proved to the universe, that, if the weakness of our Constitution, if opinion and manners did not forbid us to march to glory by the same paths as the Men, we should at least equal and sometimes surpass them in our love for public good."

Esther De Berdt Reed summarizes the goals of the Ladies' Association of Philadelphia in 1780

Left: The cover of the *Pennsylvania Magazine* in 1775 shows a woman warrior ready to fight the British.

their own families as well as people fleeing battles and armies. They were sometimes expected to give shelter to soldiers for long periods, too. The armies on both sides took food, firewood, and livestock from homes, leaving families hungry and cold.

LIFE-AND-DEATH DECISIONS

The armies brought disease, including smallpox. The chances of a family catching this fatal illness were so great that many women had their children deliberately inoculated with smallpox in the hope that they would not get too sick or die. Women had to make such life-and-death decisions themselves. Abigail Adams, who had her own children inoculated with smallpox, reflected: "It is not in the still calm of life that great characters are formed. The habits of a vigorous mind are formed in contending with difficulties. Great necessities call out great virtues."

WOMEN STEP IN

By 1780, the war was going badly for the Americans. The American troops had been routed in most battles in the North, and in 1780 the city of Charleston, South Carolina, fell to the British. American women, by this time veterans of war, felt they had to step in to help. Esther De Berdt Reed of Philadelphia described their sense of purpose in her "Sentiments of an American Woman," published in the *Pennsylvania Gazette* on June 10, 1780.

LADIES' ASSOCIATIONS

Reed formed the Ladies' Association of Philadelphia to collect money for the soldiers. Association members included Thomas Jefferson's wife, Martha Wayles Jefferson, and Benjamin Franklin's daughter, Sarah Franklin Bache.

Above: The wife of American general Philip John Schuyler sets fire to a field to prevent British troops from taking the crops.

WOMEN OF COURAGE AND CONVICTION

EMILY GEIGER (c. 1763–c. 1793)

In the summer of 1781, the Revolutionary War was still being fought fiercely in the South. The Continental Army in South Carolina, under General Nathanael Greene, was retreating from British troops under the command of Lord Rawdon. Hoping to attack the British, Greene decided to send a message to General Thomas Sumter to join him. The only person courageous enough to carry the message and risk capture by the loyalists was eighteen-year-old Emily Geiger. Under the guise of visiting her uncle, Emily rode out on horseback. She stopped at a farmhouse on the way, but the farmer alerted the British to her presence. Emily escaped through a window but was stopped by a British scouting party. She ate the message paper, so the British found nothing suspicious and let her go; but she had memorized the document's contents and was able to relay them to General Sumter.

Above: Left alone while the men are at war, a woman loads a rifle to defend her home.

Soon groups of women visited homes across Philadelphia asking for contributions, and by early July, the women had collected a large sum of money. Other ladies' associations sprang up in cities such as Trenton, New Jersey, and Baltimore, Maryland. These were the first large-scale women's associations in American history. The women hoped their efforts would show the soldiers and the world that most Americans were behind the cause of liberty.

LOYALIST WOMEN

Far less popular, but no less committed, were the loyalist women who thought that the colonies should remain part of Britain. Loyalist women sometimes took extreme measures to show the depth of their feeling—three of them plotted to kill the mayor of Albany, New York. Many loyalist women served as spies or aided the redcoats (British soldiers), providing supplies and hiding places. The women were fully aware of what they were doing and sometimes paid dearly for their loyalty to Britain by being arrested and jailed.

Ultimately, because of their political views, loyalist women and their families were forced to leave the United States. Wealthier women went to England, but most loyalists ended up in Canada. Many loyalists had followed the British army or been evacuated from such cities as New York and Charleston, South Carolina, after the war. They found themselves making their way by boat and foot through the wilds of Canada, attempting to reach small British communities. Fifty thousand loyalists settled in Canada after the war.

SLAVE WOMEN

By 1770, 47,000 slaves were living in the northern colonies and 320,000 were living in the South. The colonists were importing 4,000 slaves a year from Africa. Free black men and women lived in all the colonies, but they were in a minority. Slaves were a common sight, being unloaded from slave ships, working in northern stores and in southern wheat and tobacco fields. The slaves were treated very badly, especially in the South, where the farmwork was hard.

During the Revolutionary War, many black women could be found in American army camps, but they were slaves and did hard work such as building roads and washing uniforms. Some of the newly formed northern states, such as Vermont and Pennsylvania, prohibited slavery in their new constitutions. But plantation owners in the southern states still needed slave workers. By the end of the war, between 80,000 and 100,000 slaves had left the South, and plantations lay idle or in ruins. The laws for slaves became even

WOMEN OF COURAGE AND CONVICTION

MOLLY PITCHER (Mary Hays, 1754–1832)

Mary Hays was a camp follower in the war, traveling with her husband's regiment to cook, do the wash, and serve as a nurse. Because she brought pitchers of water to thirsty soldiers during battle, she got the nickname "Molly Pitcher." During the Battle of Monmouth, New Jersey, on June 28, 1778, Mary's husband, John Hays, was wounded and could not continue to load cannons. Mary took his place for the rest of the battle. After the war, the Pennsylvania legislature specifically gave her a pension "for her services during the Revolutionary War" rather than as the widow of a soldier, as was the custom.

Below: Molly Pitcher loads a cannon, taking the place of her wounded husband.

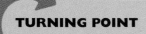

TURNING POINT

WOMEN ARE CONVICTED OF TREASON

As the war went on, more and more loyalist women were caught supporting the British government. It became clear that the women were acting on their own behalf, not just going along with what the men believed. Law statutes in the colonies changed their wording to *persons* instead of *men*, and women became responsible for political acts. After New York passed its Act of Attainder in 1779, the disloyalty of three women, Margaret Inglis, Susannah Robinson, and Mary Morris, was considered a felony and treason.

harsher since they were needed to rebuild the South—slaves were forbidden to learn to read or write and were segregated (separated) from white people.

After the start of the Revolutionary War, the British offered slaves a new opportunity for freedom. Runaway slaves were allowed to seek refuge with the British army, and many slave women ran away from southern plantations with their children to join the redcoats. At the war's end, on November 25, 1783, former slaves waited with the British loyalists to be transported to Nova Scotia and New Brunswick in Canada and to the Caribbean. Loyalists were allowed to take their slaves with them. However, even living free in their new homes, black people faced poverty and discrimination.

NATIVE AMERICAN WOMEN

Native American women, who did not see themselves or their families as either British or colonial, tried to figure out the best strategy for their own survival during the war. If the colonists won,

Right: Mohawk women and men meet in council to discuss tribal affairs. Mohawk and other Native American women lost much of their political power after the Revolution.

Native Americans would gain their independence, but it would mean that the colonists would extend their influence and move west into Native American lands. If Native American women lived among the colonists, they would also experience changes in their lifestyle and political power. In the Iroquois tribe, women had the power to select and remove chiefs and were present at councils of war. Of the Native Americans who farmed, the men hunted while the women did the farmwork. More colonists in the west would result in Native American women having to adopt the ways of white women.

At first, both the British and the colonists tried to gain the support of the Native Americans or at least get them to remain neutral. However, by 1778, the Iroquois Six Nations had split into the Mohawks, Onondagas, Cayugas, and Seneca, who fought on the side of the British, and the Oneidas and Tuscaroras, who fought on the side of the colonists. After the war, when Native American men took over agriculture from the women, they lost most of their political power in the tribes.

BREAKTHROUGH BIOGRAPHY

MOLLY (MARY) BRANDT (c. 1736–96)

Molly Brandt was a Mohawk Native American. She was educated in white schools and married William Johnson, the northern superintendent of Indian affairs for the British. Before the war, the couple had links to both the Native American and British worlds. When war broke out, Molly negotiated with the Iroquois tribe on behalf of the British, partly to help her husband and partly because she felt the British cause best served the Mohawks. Her son-in-law, Daniel Claus, said: "One word from Mary Brant [*sic*] is more taken notice of by the Five Nations than a thousand from the white man without exception." When the war ended, Molly and her family settled in Canada, where the government had given them lands in reward for their loyalty.

Below: In 1986 a Canadian postage stamp featured Molly Brandt. The three faces on the stamp represent her life as an Iroquois, a loyalist, and a European.

CHAPTER 3

WAR WORK

WHILE THE MEN WERE AWAY AT WAR, forming the new government, or seeking alliances with European countries, women kept households, farms, and businesses running. As they did so, they assumed many responsibilities for the first time and realized they could do as good a job as men. Because they were so self-reliant, they were sometimes referred to as "war widows."

Below: The women of a Revolutionary household send off to war members of the Minute Men, part of the colonial militia that responded quickly, or in minutes.

REPLACING IMPORTED GOODS

Patriot women proudly did without imported goods from Britain, such as tea and fine clothes. But essentials or near essentials, such as salt to preserve food, and pins, had to be replaced somehow. Women preserved food with walnut ash and used thorns for pins. In those times of shortages, shopkeepers who hoarded or overpriced goods risked their lives. Abigail Adams commented on a "stingy merchant"

who was overcharging for coffee in Massachusetts. A hundred or so women got together a cart and storage trunks and marched down to the store. When the merchant refused to give the women the key to the warehouse, they threw him into the cart. "Upon his finding no quarter," Abigail wrote, "he delivered the keys when they tipped up the cart and discharged him; then opened the warehouse, hoisted out the coffee themselves, put it into the trunks and drove off. . . . A large concourse of men stood amazed silent spectators." Such unified, determined action by women took place many times during the war.

FARMWORK

Colonial women had always done farmwork, but with so many men away at war, the women had to do it all, even work requiring a good deal of strength, such as mending fences around animal enclosures and cutting firewood. But the work had to be done or families risked starvation: colonial families depended on the harvest of crops and animals for their food. Few farmers in this pre-industrial time had any kind of machine, so all the work was done by hand, such as splitting wood with an ax, or with the help of animals, using them to plow the

TAKING OVER THE BUSINESS

"As I am not famous for making good Bargains in things out of my Sphere I shall put it off as long as possible, in hopes you may be at home before it is too late."

In 1777, war widow Esther Reed tried for the first time to make the important decision of exactly when to plant a crop, flax, used for making cloth. She wrote a letter to her husband describing her anxiety about this. But like many other war widows, Reed was forced to make farm decisions for herself without waiting for her husband to return.

Left: Angry Sons of Liberty or possibly soldiers and sailors in New York City tear down a statue of British king, George III on July 9, 1776.

THE RISKS OF DOING BUSINESS

"[When I established a] Publick House [for] well Accommodateing the Gentlemen of our Army . . . the Consequence . . . was, when the British took possession of that place, your Memorialist, had her House Burnt, & her Valluable Furniture Destroyed, & Rendered unable to prosecute Business."

In a petition to Congress, Rachel Farmer describes the disasters she encountered at the hands of the British when she set up a boardinghouse during the war in 1781.

BREAKTHROUGH BIOGRAPHY

BETSY ROSS (1752–1836)

Betsy Ross owned an upholstery business in Philadelphia. She knew both George and Martha Washington from church and had done sewing for George. In June 1776, George and other members of the Continental Congress asked Betsy to sew the first United States flag. He gave her a rough design for a square flag with six-pointed stars, randomly arranged. With one snip of her scissors, Betsy showed him that she could easily cut five-pointed stars and suggested arranging them in a circle on a rectangular flag. Soon the United States had its first flag, with thirteen white stars in a circle on a field of blue, and thirteen red and white stripes.

Below: Betsy Ross meets with a delegation from the Continental Congress. George Washington holds the first United States flag.

fields and other tasks. During the war, everyone who remained on the farm helped out: women, old men, and children dug potatoes, husked corn, and did whatever other work needed to be done.

Farmwork had to be done at a certain time, not when it was convenient. Cows had to be milked every morning and evening, and crops had to be harvested when they were ripe. Many farm tasks were very time consuming, and women had to do them for months or years while the men were gone. Women also still had to take care of children, cook, sew, and do the many other chores they had always done on the farm.

DECISION MAKING

For the first time, women handled the business part of farming: selling the crops for a good price, buying farm equipment and supplies, and paying workers. They bought and sold horses, settled debts, and chose which crops to plant. Sometimes, especially at first, they wrote their husbands for advice, but the mail was slow and unreliable, and women began to make an increasing number of decisions themselves, gaining confidence from their success. "What was done, was done by myself," proudly declared farm wife Azubah Norton of Connecticut.

Above: Women worked hard in colonial times. A time-consuming chore was drawing water from a well for drinking, washing, and watering gardens. When the men left for war, women took over whatever else had to be done for the home and farm.

ATTENDING TO MATTERS

Sarah Frazier described in later years how her grandmother ran the family farm during the Revolutionary War. "All the cloth and linen that my Grandfather wore during the war were spun at home, most of it by her own hands," she wrote. "All the clothing of the family (and it was not a small one) during this time was made at home except weaving. All the business of every kind, she attended to Farm, Iron Works, and domestic matters. In Summer as soon as it was light she had her horse saddled, rode over the farm and directed the men about their work, often rode down to the creek, where Sharpless' Iron Works are now, and was back at breakfast

THE ROLE OF NURSES

"The nurses . . . administer the medicine and diet prescribed for the sick according to order; they obey all orders they receive from the Matron; not only to be attentive to the cleanliness of the wards and patients but to keep themselves clean. . . . They are to see that every patient, upon his admission into the Hospital is immediately washed with warm water, that his face and hands are washed and head combed every morning."

George Washington in 1778

WOMEN OF COURAGE AND CONVICTION

ABIGAIL ADAMS (1744–1818)

Abigail Adams was born in Weymouth, Massachusetts, and educated at home, where she taught herself how to read French. She married John Adams on October 25, 1764. They lived on a farm in Braintree, Massachusetts, where even before the war Abigail was usually in charge. She made the decisions on what crops to plant and the prices to ask for them while John pursued a career as a lawyer. As war approached, Adams, an ardent patriot, wrote British historian Catharine Sawbridge Macaulay: "The only alternative which every American thinks of is liberty or death." While John Adams was away during the war years on Continental Congress business, Abigail managed the family and businesses, sometimes for years at a time. When her husband became president of the United States in 1797, Abigail's knowledge of world affairs and her intelligent interest in politics equipped her well to converse with visiting dignitaries.

time to give her attention and toil to the children, servants, & household affairs."

James Warren, the husband of author Mercy Otis Warren, visited Abigail Adams during the war at the family's farm in Braintree, Massachusetts. "Mrs. Adams Native genius will Excel us all in Husbandry," Warren wrote. "She was much Engaged when I came along, and the Farm At Braintree Appeared to be Under Excellent Management."

OUR FARMING BUSINESS

Mary Bartlett was the wife of Josiah Bartlett, a New Hampshire congressman who stayed in Philadelphia for much of the war. When Josiah first went to Congress in the fall of 1775, he wrote his wife that he hoped she would have "no Great trouble about my out Door affairs" and referred to "my farming Business." By 1776, Mary was still referring to "your Business" in her letters, but by 1778, she wrote confidently of "our farming business."

TAKING CHARGE

Women also took over other businesses their husbands had run or they continued in the jobs they had always held.

Below: A loyalist woman elegantly entertains British soldiers on her porch during the Revolution.

Some women, especially single women or widows, had always run their own businesses. These included dry goods, liquor, or grocery stores; boardinghouses, taverns, or inns; dressmaker or hatmaker shops; teaching; and midwifery. Some women, short of money in men's absence, went to work for the first time.

The war benefited some women's businesses. In Philadelphia, where the Continental Congress met, the delegates rented many rooms in boardinghouses. Some landladies rented rooms to officers and soldiers and were paid to cook meals for them. Sick and wounded soldiers were sometimes sent to boardinghouses for care.

YOUR GOOD MANAGEMENT

In time, men began to trust women to run family businesses well. Away from home for years, the men, especially officers in the army and those appointed to Congress, had no choice. To

Below: In the movie *The Patriot*, Anne Howard, played by Lisa Brenner, reluctantly says goodbye to her husband, Gabriel Martin, played by Heath Ledger, as he returns to war.

A DREARY DESERT

"I feel forlorn & desolate, & the World appears like a dreary Desart, almost without any visible protecting Hand to guard us from the ravenous Wolves & Lions that prowl about for prey."

Left in charge of her home in September 1777, Sally Fisher describes the unbearable weight of her responsibilities.

BEARING UP

"[I have] been enabled to bear up thro' every triall & difficulty far beyond what I could have expected."

By November 1777, Sally Fisher tells how she has coped with the task she has been set. When Fisher's husband returned in April 1778, she became an active participant in the discussions about household finances.

begin with, men's letters home contained specific instructions to their wives, but later on they offered more general statements. One man wrote: "I Can't give any Other Directions About Home more than what I have Done but must Leave all to your good Management."

BREAKTHROUGH BIOGRAPHY

MARY GODDARD (1738–1816)

Mary Goddard began her career as a printer in 1762 in Providence, Rhode Island, where her brother had a printing shop. In 1774, she moved to Baltimore, Maryland, to take over a new printing shop and newspaper, the *Maryland Journal*. Mary's brother described her as "an expert and correct compositor of types." The masthead of the May 10, 1775, issue carried her name and read: "Published by M. K. Goddard." In 1775, Benjamin Franklin appointed Mary Goddard the postmaster of Baltimore. She was the first woman to hold a federal office. In December 1776, the Continental Congress asked her to print the first official version of the Declaration of Independence. In October 1789, Mary lost the postmaster job to a man, although two hundred Baltimore businessmen had endorsed her petition to keep her position. For the rest of her life, she ran a bookshop in Baltimore.

Right: Mary Goddard's almanac included subjects such as fables, court decisions, and astronomy.

EQUAL COMMAND

As women became confident in their abilities to manage businesses, they started to expect greater respect and the right to be included in family decision making. Lucy Flucker Knox, the wife of a high-ranking official in the colonial army, was forced to leave her home in Manhattan after British general William Howe landed with his troops on Long Island in the summer of 1776. She chose to go to New Haven rather than Fairfield, Connecticut, which her husband had advised. Her husband wrote angrily that she was no better than most women, "trifling insignificant Animals," but quickly apologized after receiving an even angrier response from Lucy. By March 1777, Lucy was describing herself as "quite a woman of business" and wrote in a letter to her husband, "I hope you will not consider yourself as commander in chief of your own house—but be convinced . . . that there is such a thing as equal command."

Some women continued with age-old occupations, such as midwifery. Commonly, in Revolutionary times, a pregnant woman would have a midwife to assist in the birth of her child. Delivering babies was considered mostly a job for women, and doctors were scarce in the countryside. Modern medicine, with its painkillers and antibiotics (or even thermometers), did not exist, and a midwife usually could do as much or more for a woman as a doctor. The midwife was often also a healer, preparing medicines for neighbors from plants. Martha Moore Ballard, a grandmother in Augusta, Maine, lived on a farm during Revolutionary times and worked hard as a midwife, delivering more than a thousand babies in twenty-five years. She kept up the traditions of baking, preserving, sewing, and making soap for her family. Another midwife, Janet Cumming, a widow living in Charleston, South Carolina, made as much money as a merchant or lawyer.

Above: In Revolutionary times, women relied on midwives to deliver their babies.

CHAPTER 4

WOMEN AND POLITICS

URING THE REVOLUTIONARY WAR, A FEW WOMEN, such as Abigail Adams and Mercy Otis Warren, had voiced strong political opinions. Other women had formed societies that expanded their political awareness and given them the opportunity to become involved in activities outside the home. During the postwar years, the number of women's service and reform societies geared toward improving the republic increased. The main thrust of these organizations was improvement through good example, based on domestic virtues.

SELF-GOVERNMENT

Once the war ended on September 3, 1783, with the signing of the Treaty of Paris in Paris, France, the citizens of the new country, now called the United States, were ready to begin governing themselves. They took the task very seriously. Although they had triumphed in the war with Britain, the most powerful country in the world might not stay vanquished for long. Also, the success of the new country was by no means guaranteed. Its system of government, blending English common law and Roman law, had to work for the special circumstances of the United States—a brand-new nation with vast amounts of unsettled land and many different nationalities of people living together.

THE ADAMS LETTERS

Women were just as concerned as men about shaping the new republic. Abigail Adams wrote many thoughtful and

Left: Abigail Adams, the second first lady of the United States.

26

insightful letters to her husband, John, about how the new country should be structured. One of her letters contained her famous appeal to him to "remember the ladies" in the country's Constitution, which set out the laws of the United States.

In his reply to Abigail's "remember the ladies" letter, John Adams probably took the view of most of the founding fathers who were writing the Constitution. He dismissed his wife's concerns about women's legal rights in the new country, giving two reasons to support his argument. First, too many other groups of people without rights, such as Native Americans and slaves, were also asking for greater equality in the new country. Too many people asking for too much would result in loss of control and chaos. Second, he argued that in truth, women controlled men, albeit indirectly.

POWER OVER WIVES

Abigail continued to pursue her case for women's rights in her letters to John, writing on May 7, 1776, "I cannot say that I think you are very

TURNING POINT

AFRICAN-AMERICAN BENEVOLENT SOCIETIES

From 1790 on, African-American women formed organizations for mutual aid. Members contributed money to be given to sick members for food and to others in need. Two such organizations were the Female Benevolent Society of St. Thomas, formed in 1793, and the Daughters of Africa, formed in about 1821.

FRONTISPIECE.

Thackara & Vallance sculp.

Publish'd at Philada Decr 1st 1792.

WOMEN OF COURAGE AND CONVICTION

MARY WOLLSTONECRAFT (1759–97)

Mary Wollstonecraft was British, but her novels and political works had a great effect on American women's thinking in the late 18th and early 19th centuries. Her book *Vindication on the Rights of Women* (1792) argued strongly against the superiority of men. Some women agreed with Mary's ideas but not with the strong language she used to convey them. Wollstonecraft recognized that most women would marry and have children, and the proper training of "affectionate wives and mothers" was an important theme in her writing. Her novel *Mary, a Fiction* (1788) portrayed a woman who sought love outside of marriage. Mary Wollstonecraft lived a radical lifestyle for the time, conceiving two children out of wedlock. She died in childbirth; her daughter, Mary Shelley, achieved fame as the author of the novel *Frankenstein*.

Left: In the British *Lady's Magazine*, the "Genius" of the magazine presents "Liberty" with a copy of Mary Wollstonecraft's book *Vindication on the Rights of Women*.

"REMEMBER THE LADIES"

"I long to hear that you have declared an independency. . . . In the new code of laws. . . . I desire you would remember the ladies and be more generous and favorable to them than your ancestors. Do not put such unlimited power into the hands of the husbands. Remember, all men would be tyrants if they could. If particular care and attention is not paid to the ladies, we are determined to foment a rebellion, and will not hold ourselves bound by any laws in which we have not voice or representation."

From a letter by Abigail Adams to her husband, John Adams, March 31, 1776

generous to the ladies; for, whilst you are proclaiming peace and good-will to men, emancipating all nations, you insist upon retaining an absolute power over wives. But you must remember that arbitrary power is like most other things which are very hard, very liable to be broken; and, notwithstanding all your wise laws and maxims, we have it in our power, not only to free ourselves, but to subdue our masters, and, without violence, throw both your natural and legal authority at our feet."

But Abigail did not have her way in getting women's rights specifically included in the Constitution. She would later write, in 1782: "Patriotism in the female sex is the most disinterested of all virtues" since women felt it so strongly although they

Below: John Trumbull's famous painting shows the drafting committee presenting its work on the Declaration of Independence to Congress in 1776. John Adams is standing in the center in a brown suit. Abigail and John Adams exchanged many letters during this period, when John was away in Philadelphia during the Continental congresses.

were "excluded from honours and from offices" and "deprived of a voice in legislation, obliged to submit to those laws which are imposed upon [them]."

DECLARATION OF INDEPENDENCE

Women were not specifically excluded in the country's first document to describe equality and rights in the United States, but the issue of women's rights was not addressed either. The Declaration of Independence was written by third president Thomas Jefferson and adopted by Congress on July 4, 1776. It stated the intention of the thirteen American colonies to separate from Britain and form a separate country. It did not specifically mention women among those declaring

ANOTHER TRIBE

"As to your extraordinary code of laws, I cannot but laugh. We have been told that our struggle has loosened the bands of government everywhere; that children and apprentices were disobedient; that schools and colleges were grown turbulent; that Indians slighted their guardians, and negroes grew insolent to their masters. But your letter was the first intimation that another tribe, more numerous and powerful than all the rest, were grown discontented. . . . Depend upon it, we know better than to repeal our masculine systems. Although they are in full force, you know they are little more than theory. We dare not exert our power in its full latitude. We are obliged to go fair and softly, and, in practice, you know we are the subjects. We have only the name of masters."

On April 14, 1776, John Adams replied to Abigail about her proposed code of laws.

Left: John Adams, second president of the United States. His lively letters to Abigail are a good record of how men in power felt about women's rights after the Revolution.

ALL MEN ARE EQUAL

"When, in the course of human events, it becomes necessary for one people to dissolve the political bonds which have connected them with another, and to assume among the powers of the earth, the separate and equal station to which the laws of nature and of nature's God entitle them, a decent respect to the opinions of mankind requires that they should declare the causes which impel them to the separation.

"We hold these truths to be self-evident, that all men are created equal, that they are endowed by their Creator with certain unalienable rights, that among these are life, liberty and the pursuit of happiness."

The Declaration of Independence includes all people, men and women, in its sweeping opening statement of the reasons for establishing the United States. But women, African Americans, and Native Americans would have to wait for many years for the Declaration's promises to be fulfilled.

themselves in the document. Although the words *mankind* and *men* are used, that was the convention of the time, and the words *human* and *people* also appear.

LEGAL RIGHTS

In the late 18th and early 19th centuries, women had few legal rights. Under English common law, which still applied in the

Right: The U.S. Constitution was the result of the Constitutional Convention held between May and September 1787. Here George Washington, Benjamin Franklin, and other founding fathers greet an excited crowd at the Convention, which was held in the State House in Philadelphia, the same place the Declaration of Independence was signed.

Left: In this illustration, women are advised to keep within the compass of good behavior to avoid any troubles that may be lurking.

TURNING POINT

NEW JERSEY GIVES THE VOTE TO WOMEN

The thirteen new states adopted state constitutions to supplement the national Constitution. New Jersey's constitution, adopted on July 2, 1776, was unique since it gave the vote to all free inhabitants of legal age who met property and residency standards. Unfortunately, by 1807 the legislature had passed a law restricting the right to vote to white males with property. The reason given was, "It is highly necessary to the safety, quiet, good order, and dignity of the state."

American colonies, women lost most of their legal rights when they married. Any money or property a woman owned when she married became her husband's to control. Married women could not make a will, vote, hold office, or sit on a jury. Single women had more rights than married women. However, before the explosion of job opportunities that occurred at the time of the Industrial Revolution, few women could afford to remain single when hardly any jobs for them existed outside the home. Strict divorce laws made it almost impossible to end a marriage. In the rare instances when divorce did occur, the woman generally had to give up legal control of her children, and lost her home. Many women hoped that under the new Constitution of the United States, which outlined how the country would be governed, they would get more legal rights.

To the disappointment of Abigail Adams and many other women, the Constitution, which was ratified from 1787 to 1790 by the thirteen former colonies (now states) did not give women specific rights. Like the Declaration of Independence, the Constitution did not specifically limit those rights. African Americans did not get equal rights until the Constitution was amended after the Civil War (1861–65), and Native American men and women did not become United States citizens until the Citizenship Act of 1924.

THE CONSTITUTION

The Constitution of the United States was the next document to set out human social and political rights in the new country. Adopted on September 17, 1787, by the Constitutional Convention in Philadelphia,

"

CONSTITUTIONAL RIGHTS

"We the People of the United States, in Order to form a more perfect Union, establish Justice, insure domestic Tranquility, provide for the common defence, promote the general Welfare, and secure the Blessings of Liberty to ourselves and our Posterity, do ordain and establish this Constitution for the United States of America. . . . "

"(Representatives and direct Taxes shall be apportioned among the several States which may be included within this Union, according to their respective Numbers, which shall be determined by adding to the whole Number of free Persons, including those bound to Service for a Term of Year, and excluding Indians not taxed, three fifths of all other Persons.)"

The Constitution, setting out the laws of the new United States, began by speaking for all of its people. Yet the Constitution went on to limit the rights of African Americans and Native Americans.

Right: The U.S. Constitution gave sweeping rights to white men but left out or discriminated against other groups, especially slaves.

Pennsylvania, and ratified by each of the thirteen states, the Constitution began: "We the People" and went on to describe the three branches of government—the executive, the legislative, and the judicial—and who would get to vote in the United States. Article I, Section 2, Clause 3 of the Constitution excluded Native Americans and slaves from voting but did not specifically refer to women. Since in those days a person had to own property to vote, most women could not have voted anyway. The Constitution did leave the door open for women to get full political rights by not specifically excluding them—but because the laws of individual states subsequently denied women the vote and other rights, women could not vote in the United States until Congress passed the 19th Amendment to the U.S. Constitution in 1920.

WOMEN'S WRITING

Despite not being able to vote, women began in increasing numbers to influence the course of their new country by the power of the pen, persuading others to support the country and defining the behavior of the new republican woman. A new form of patriotic literature appeared, including works by playwright, poet, and historian Mercy Otis Warren, essayist and political thinker Judith Sargent Murray, and many others. The women writers expected that they would be heard, and their works were widely read.

During the war, women's writing both to relatives and for publication had emphasized the need to support the cause for independence, which would lead to personal freedom and the freedom for the country to govern itself. After the war, women wanted to show in their writings how the republic could be preserved—and many authors, both men and women, thought that women would be responsible for this through their own virtue and their example to men and children.

BREAKTHROUGH BIOGRAPHY

MERCY OTIS WARREN (1728–1814)

Mercy Otis Warren was a playwright, poet, and historian. In her writings, she championed the cause of independence and reflected at length on the meaning and future of the American Revolution. She married James Warren, a general in George Washington's army, in 1754. She wrote several plays with political themes, including *The Group*, which appeared in 1775, just before the Battle of Lexington. The Group was the name Warren gave to the loyalists who were at that time administering Boston, and her play painted a very unflattering portrait of them. In 1790, she published *Poems, Dramatic and Miscellaneous*, the first work under her own name. For the next twenty years, she worked on her three-volume *History of the Rise, Progress, and Termination of the American Revolution*, which expressed her republican, democratic views.

Below: Mercy Otis Warren reflected deeply in her writings on the meaning of the Revolution.

CHAPTER 5

INDUSTRY AND WORK

THE INDUSTRIAL REVOLUTION MEANT THAT WOMEN and men who had been occupied in cottage industries or farming suddenly moved to towns and cities in search of work in the new mills and factories. Factory work was tough and exhausting, and conditions were often unhealthy. Nevertheless, some women found a new sense of independence in working outside the home and earning their own living.

Below: The Blackstone River powered the machines in the spinning and carding mill at Pawtucket, Rhode Island.

THE SPINNING FRAME

An enormous change to the lives of American women came from Britain in the form of a new, improved spinning frame invented by Richard Arkwright, who built his first textile mill in Cromford, England, in 1774. Arkwright's

Above: Emigrants cross the Appalachian Mountains on their way to Pittsburgh, Pennsylvania, in search of new jobs in the city.

spinning frame produced stronger thread for yarn. It was automatic, water powered (water wheels turned the machinery), and worked continuously. This textile machine made possible the move away from small home production of yarns to production in factories. On December 20, 1790, Samuel Slater began to operate water-powered machinery for spinning and carding cotton in Pawtucket, Rhode Island, in a mill built on the Blackstone River. The Slater mill was the first American factory to produce cotton yarn successfully with water-powered machines.

THE MOVE TO THE CITIES

Many other areas of production in the United States had become industrialized. Farms became bigger, and farmers sold crops for cash instead of producing just enough for the family's needs. More and more people moved to cities and, instead of working at home at crafts such as furniture making, began working for businesses outside the home. Farms still supplied part of families' needs, but increasingly a farm wife would buy such items as spices, teacups, nails, and paper at a store.

TURNING POINT

WOMEN BECOME SHOPPERS

In colonial America, women had made most of the products they needed at home, such as cloth, bread, and soap. Usually the man of the family had shopped for whatever store-bought goods the family needed, such as furniture. In the late 18th and early 19th centuries, women began to do more shopping, especially for clothes and food. An increasing number of men worked for wages, so their families had more money to spend on store-bought items. Women didn't have to spend as much of their day making essentials at home and therefore had more time to spare.

TURNING POINT

"ON THE CLOCK"

In colonial times, before factory work, people's working lives were governed by irregular hours, determined by the weather, when the harvest was ripe, and other unpredictable factors. As American society moved to modern industrial work patterns, family production was replaced by wage earning, natural rhythms were replaced by the regularity of machines, and workplaces became separated from the home. The working day consisted of a fixed number of hours, for which workers started and finished at a set time each day. Traditional women's work, such as cooking, sewing, and child care, remained "off the clock." At first, many women who took jobs outside the home had difficulty adjusting to a rigid schedule.

Above: Slave women still had to work at hard jobs for no pay after the Revolution.

WORK OUTSIDE THE HOME

Increasingly, both men and women worked for wages outside the home. Poor, black, or immigrant women already worked outside the home for low wages, but in the early 19th century other women joined the workforce. In 1814, Francis Cabot Lowell set up the first power loom in the United States to spin thread and weave cloth in one factory in Waltham, Massachusetts. He hired single farm girls to tend the power-driven machines. His reason for doing so was that the girls were disciplined, cheap, and would not compete with skilled workmen. More textile mills, the first factories in America, were set up in New England. Soon the building of mills spread rapidly across the country, and each mill owner hired women workers. As a result, during the early part of the 19th century, the number of women working outside the home for wages rose greatly.

NEW OPPORTUNITY

Women had the opportunity to work for wages in textile factories, and they took it. Poorer women were glad to earn money to support themselves and their families. Many women wrote home that they liked their new work, although they usually didn't work for long. Most worked for a few years while young and single before marrying and giving up work outside the home. They might give the money they made to their families to help pay off debts or to send brothers or (in rare instances) sisters to school, or they might save it.

REGULATION PAPER

To work in a mill, a woman had to sign a "regulation paper" promising that she would go to church regularly, observe strict moral behavior, and live in a boardinghouse associated with the factory. The requirements were intended to protect the young women, but they were also designed to keep them under control and ensure they observed regular hours so that they were more productive.

WORKING CONDITIONS

Women's work in the cotton and woolen mills was not at all like modern-day factory or office work. Women might work 12½-to-16-hour days, and they were not paid as much as men for the same work.

Below: The mill at Lowell, Massachusetts, home to the "moral police," set itself the task of keeping female mill workers virtuous.

THE MORAL POLICE

"*[Without moral guidance, the] profits would be absorbed by cases of irregularity, carelessness, and neglect; while the existence of any great moral exposure in Lowell would cut off the supply of help from the virtuous homesteads of the country. . . . The sagacity of self-interest, as well as more disinterested considerations, has led to the adoption of a strict system of moral police.*"

Henry Miles, a clergyman in the mill town of Lowell, Massachusetts, outlines his reasons for applying restrictions to the freedom of workers. Mill owners believed they needed their female employees to be reliable and chaste.

TURNING POINT

MARY PICKERSGILL'S FLAG

During the summer of 1813, Major George Armistead, the new commander of Fort McHenry, commissioned Mary Pickersgill to make a U.S. flag to fly above the fort, which guarded the city of Baltimore, Maryland. Mary, who came from a family of flag makers, undertook the task. When finished, the giant flag measured 30 feet by 42 feet. On September 14, 1814, Francis Scott Key, held prisoner by the British aboard ship, watched anxiously through the night as the British attacked Baltimore to see which flag flew over Fort McHenry: the Union Jack (the British flag) or the Stars and Stripes. At dawn, he saw that "our flag was still there" and on the back of a letter wrote the words to "The Star-Spangled Banner," which became the national anthem of the United States.

Rght: Work in the mills could be tedious, but many women liked the independence their jobs gave them. Also, unlike farmwork, mill jobs sometimes allowed workers to sit down and the hours, though long, were regular.

In the boardinghouses, as many as twelve women might sleep in one room; much of their wages went to pay for board. They could easily be dismissed for immoral conduct, bad language, disrespect, or even attending dancing classes. Being fired from one mill meant being blacklisted from all other mills.

Some women described the boardinghouses as pleasant places, with pianos, libraries, and carpeted parlors. The boarders might spend their evenings reading, sewing, or writing letters. The young women working in the mills led very different lives from their mothers, who still continued their old lifestyles of managing the household and caring for children.

A USEFUL CONTRIBUTION

Men sometimes supported the practice of women's work outside the home. In 1791, Secretary of the Treasury Alexander Hamilton, in his

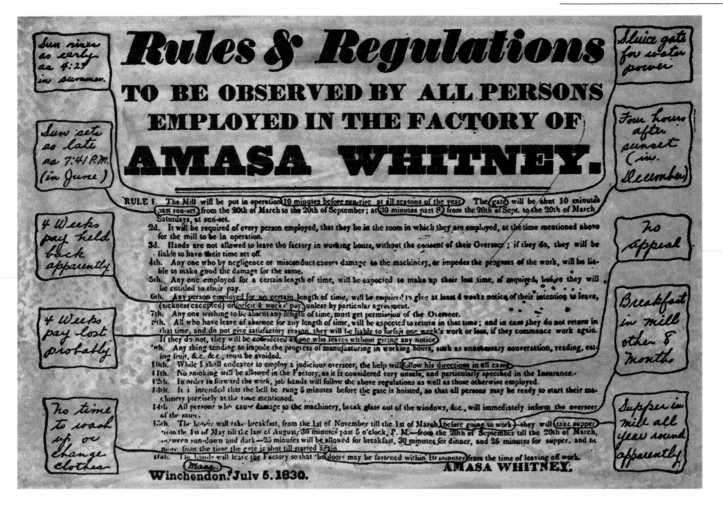

Above: The Rules and Regulations at the Amasa Whitney factory in Winchendon, Massachusetts, prescribed working hours from sunrise to sunset, prohibited smoking, set a penalty of lost wages for pauses and absences on the job, and placed many other restrictions on the workers.

"Report on Manufactures," encouraged women to work in factories. Women could then add to the family's income, he wrote, and those who might otherwise be dependent on the community for support would be "rendered more useful."

ORGANIZING AND PROTESTING

One effect of so many women working together for the first time was that a lot of them joined women's organizations. To begin with, young women in their first jobs, away from home for the first time, accepted low pay and poor working conditions in the mills. But soon they began to organize and demand better treatment. In the Pawtucket mills in 1824, 102 female textile workers were angered by wage cuts and increased work hours. They walked out with their male co-workers and were the first women to join a strike. In 1828, new rules at the mills, such as a ban on talking during work and on unions, 12½-cent fines for lateness, and a reduction of wages from 58 to 53 cents a day caused 800 "mill girls" to walk off the job, march around the factory with banners and signs, and set off fireworks. The mill owners simply advertised

BREAKTHROUGH BIOGRAPHY

REBECCA LUKENS
(1794–1854)

Educated at a boarding school, Rebecca Lukens took over the Brandywine Iron Works in Coatesville, Pennsylvania, as manager and owner after the death of her husband, who had run the company. With her brother supervising day-to-day operations, Rebecca got the company out of debt and repaired its facilities. She then continued to supervise the production of boilers and hulls for steamboats and later on iron parts for railroad steam locomotives. The company flourished under Rebecca's leadership and continued to operate after her death, becoming Bethlehem Steel.

Right: After the Revolution, Rebecca Lukens managed the company that became Bethlehem Steel, once the second-largest steel producer in the United States.

for four hundred replacements. Afraid of losing their jobs, the women returned to work, but the groundwork had been laid for more effective strikes later on.

PAID WORK AT HOME

Before the Revolutionary War, women had sometimes sold or traded items such as butter, cheese, or cloth with neighbors. Young women in particular might have helped in another household for pay. As the United States became more industrialized, many women were paid by companies to do piecework at home. The stitching and binding of boots and shoes and the braiding of straw bonnets were two kinds of work done by many women in New England for wages. Women also rented rooms for other workers to board in their homes. Increasingly, wages were needed to buy essentials. In 1797, Abigail Lyman, a woman living in Boston, remarked: "There is no way of living in this town without cash."

RICH WOMEN

Then as now, a small number of women were wealthy enough not to have to work, either for wages or in the home. These women spent their days receiving and making visits, reading novels, painting or playing the piano, attending church and lectures, shopping, taking walks, attending charity organization meetings, going to dances, and learning French.

However, the lack of industry could be unsatisfying. Amelia Lee Jackson of Boston wrote when she was twenty-one: "I think a girl's life at my age isn't the most pleasant by any means; she is in the most unsettled state: a young man can occupy himself with his business, and look forward to his life and prospects, but all we have to do is to pass our time agreeably to ourselves. . . . I think everyone likes to feel the *necessity* of doing something, and I confess that I have sometimes wished I could be poor to have the pleasure of exerting my self."

THE CHARMS OF HOME

In the early 1800s, women had more choices about what to do with their lives than in colonial times. Some preferred to remain at home, doing traditional work. Anna Bryant Smith of Portland, Maine, worked in her husband's store behind the counter when needed and picked out goods for the store when she and her husband traveled to Boston. But Anna preferred work at home to work at the store. "A Storm is most welcome," she wrote in January 1807, "for then I stay at home which has more charms for me than any other place." Anna liked to work at home even though she listed many chores she had to do there: washing dishes, cleaning, making beds, cooking meals, weaving and sewing, baking bread, preserving fruit, brewing beer, curing bacon, making candles, and knitting.

Below: Whether for the family or wages, women continued to sew in their homes after the Revolution.

CHAPTER 6

EDUCATION

DURING THIS ERA, THE EDUCATION OF GIRLS WAS secondary to that of boys. Women were valued for their "accomplishments"; for example, their ability to speak a foreign language or play an instrument. Many poorer women, however, went through their lives not learning how to read or write, and slaves had no education at all.

HOMESCHOOLING

Before the Revolutionary War, most women did not receive much in the way of education. A history of Puritanism meant that many people had stern ideas about girls' education. They believed God had ordained that women should devote themselves to domestic responsibilities and not meddle in the "male" sphere of ideas and learning. The country was sparsely populated, and there was no public school system. Children were often taught to read and write at home by parents or an older sibling. More than half of the women in New England in the 18th century could not even sign their names.

ACCOMPLISHMENTS

Those girls who did receive an education were usually taught at small schools run by women, often out of their homes. At these places, girls learned "accomplishments" such as music,

Left: An increasing number of women were themselves educated, and they kept their responsibilities for the education and care of children.

dancing, and French. Girls might go to several different establishments to learn different accomplishments; for example, one school for sewing and another for writing. Such schools were in cities, which generally meant that farm girls lived too far away to attend. Tutors, hired to teach boys in wealthy plantation families in the South, might also teach the girls of the family. Poor southern girls were taught only by their families, if at all. Occasionally girls were sent to schools for boys and taught in a separate room for shorter hours or during the summer.

Girls' education seldom extended farther than accomplishments; its usual purpose was to make women seem more desirable as wives. Colleges such as Harvard and Yale were not open to women. Abigail Adams wrote to a male acquaintance in 1778 that she found it "mortifying" to see "the difference of education between the male and female sex, even in those families where education is attended to."

SUPPORTING THE REPUBLIC

Women had ably run households and businesses during the war. Afterward they were put in charge of raising the next generation of patriotic, competent women and men to preserve the republic. To do that, almost everyone agreed, women needed a better education. During the war, Abigail Adams wrote to John Adams: "Much depends . . . upon

GIRLS' INSTRUCTION

"Mrs. Woodbury announces that she will open a boarding school for young ladies at her house on Market St. where instruction will be given in the French and English languages, drawing, embroidery, etc."

An advertisement for a school in Newburyport, Massachusetts, from the *Impartial Herald* in 1791 describes the teaching of accomplishments at a school for young ladies.

THE GOALS OF A GIRL'S EDUCATION

"Usefulness should be the result of education, the great object of future life. . . . [Education should] inspire virtuous sentiments [in women] . . . . Though women are not destined to the commotions of public life, or to act in those professions, which hold forth a stimulus to the exertions of the other sex, it is still necessary that they be taught the value of knowledge, and instructed in a taste for literary pursuits."

Nancy Maria Hyde, a teacher at a school in Hartford, Connecticut, wrote down her thoughts about the education of young women in 1816.

Left: Both women and men agreed on the importance of education for children so that they would be good citizens of the new republic.

Right: After the Revolution, daughters had more options in life than their mothers had before them.

NEGLECTING EDUCATION

"In this country you need not be told how much female education is neglected, nor how fashionable it has been to ridicule female learning."

In 1778, during the Revolution, while John Adams was composing the Constitution of the United States with the other founding fathers, his wife Abigail wrote to him about the importance of women's education.

the early education of youth, and the first principles which are instilled take the deepest root. . . . If we mean to have heroes, statesmen, and philosophers, we should have learned women."

SENSIBLE AND INFORMED

Judith Sargent Murray wrote in her essay column "The Gleaner" in Boston after the war that girls should be taught to think, "to reason, investigate, and compare, and to invigorate their understandings by a comprehension, and a consequent adoption of those arguments which result from sound sense, and are recognized by truth." Ideally, education would produce "a Sensible and informed woman—companionable and serious—possessing also a facility of temper, and united to a congenial mind—blest with competency—rearing to maturity a promising family of children."

Most schools for young women taught a mix of accomplishments and academic subjects. The goal of these establishments was to broaden women's knowledge to an extent, but not to create full-fledged citizens who voted, worked alongside men outside the home, and participated as equals in political discussions.

NEW SCHOOLS

Hundreds of private academies for girls opened after the Revolutionary War, and an increasing number of American families paid for their daughters to attend. For the first time, girls were taught reading, composition (essay writing), rhetoric (speaking effectively), math, history, the sciences, art, music, and even Greek and Latin. Younger girls were not excluded from the school reform movement: the number of primary, or elementary, schools also increased in the United States. In Massachusetts, towns used tax money to support the schools.

A DAUGHTER'S DAILY SCHEDULE

"from 8. to 10 o'clock practice music.
from 10. to 1. dance one day and draw another.
from 1. to 2. draw on the day you dance, and write a letter the next day.
from 3. to 4. read French.
from 4. to 5. exercise yourself in music.
from 5. till bedtime read English, write &c."

Thomas Jefferson, a widower, wrote to his ten-year-old daughter Patsy on November 28, 1783, instructing her to keep to a strict schedule while he was away on business.

Below: Many schools continued to teach accomplishments, such as playing the piano, to young women.

Above: The Troy Female Seminary, founded by Emma Willard in Troy, New York, took education for women to a higher level than previous schools—Willard taught all subjects in the seminary, not just traditionally female-oriented ones.

Many graduates of the new academies did become teachers, opening up a new career for women.

Previous girls' schools had been small, often with just one teacher holding classes in her home; the new schools hired many teachers and had permanent buildings. Many of the academies were in small towns and accepted boarding pupils from around the country. Wealthy girls from the South, which recovered slowly from the war, had to attend school in the North. Wealthy or middle-class women could afford to attend these schools, but poor women could not. Slave women were not permitted an education.

TROY FEMALE SEMINARY

In September 1821, Emma Willard, a product of the republican female academies for women, opened the Troy Female Seminary in Troy, New York, with ninety girls in the first class. She had planned carefully for the school, getting the backing of many powerful men of the time, including Thomas Jefferson, John Adams, and Governor George Clinton of New York. The Troy Female Seminary was the first public school for women funded by the government, the Common Council of Troy, New York.

EQUALITY WITH MEN

Willard hoped the school would educate women differently from other American schools, bringing "its subjects to the perfection of their moral, intellectual and physical nature: in order that they may be the means of the greatest possible happiness of which they are capable, both as to what they enjoy and what they communicate." The school had another purpose: to put women on terms of equality with men. "Reason and religion teach that we too are primary existences . . . the companions, not the satellites of men," Willard wrote.

Willard was an advocate of women becoming teachers, stating that they were naturally inclined to teach and pointing out that they would be satisfied with lower pay than men. A teacher herself, she thought that students should learn the history of their own country first and wrote an American history textbook to replace classical history texts about ancient Greece and Rome. She taught students geography through drawing a map of their hometown.

NEW EDUCATION FOR A NEW COUNTRY

A school such as Willard's not only raised the level of women's intellectual achievement but also changed the relation between men and women. Such a revolutionary enterprise needed to be handled with tact. Abigail Adams, Judith Sargent Murray, Emma Willard, and many other women who wanted these changes argued their case in writing. They emphasized that they were not suggesting women compete with men in any way or that men might not support educational reform for women. They justified the introduction of higher education for women by saying it was a woman's duty to raise responsible citizens for the republic. The training of

> ### BREAKTHROUGH BIOGRAPHY
>
> #### EMMA WILLARD (1787–1870)
>
> By the time Emma Willard was thirteen, she had taught herself geometry, philosophy, literature, and arithmetic.
> A successful teacher, in 1814 she attempted to enroll at Middlebury College in Vermont but was rejected since the college admitted only men. She decided to open her own school for women, the Troy Female Seminary, teaching college-level classes. It was the world's first academy for women and the first school to teach women science, philosophy, history, and other subjects previously taught only to men. In 1895, the school, which still exists, was renamed the Emma Willard School.

Below: Emma Willard encouraged women to reach their full potential in her school.

▶ **BREAKTHROUGH BIOGRAPHY**

CATHARINE SEDGWICK (1789–1867)

Catharine Sedgwick was considered a founder of American literature, along with such famous authors as Washington Irving and James Fenimore Cooper. She was educated formally at Payne's Finishing School in New York and privately in several languages. Sedgwick wrote several novels, short stories, children's books, travelogs, journals, and biographies, helping to create a new form of American literature that combined historical events with romantic themes. She was known for her courageous female characters and her descriptions of local, New England natural beauty and people's dress. Her first novel, *A New-England Tale: Or, Sketches of New-England Character and Manners* (1822), tells the tale of a young orphaned Quaker living in rural New England and the cruelty to her of supposedly pious relatives. Sedgwick's novel *Hope Leslie* (1827), a sympathetic portrayal of an English colonist who marries a Native American, made Sedgwick the most famous American writer of her time.

Right: Catharine Marie Sedgwick (1789–1867) was a pathbreaking novelist in the early United States.

aristocratic European women in colonial times would give way to the education of a wider range of American women, a move that could also be seen as appropriate for the new country.

THE IMPORTANCE OF MOTHERS

All Americans agreed that mothers in the new republic should be well educated. In 1811, voicing a common opinion, Mary Jackson Lee wrote to her sister about a niece: "You wish her heart to be more richly cultivated than the head, and this cannot be under any one's tuition so well as yours. A mother alone can do this, I believe."

The new female academies, with their serious courses of study, replaced the informal instruction in accomplishments, showing that

the academies were the right path for a republic. As the academies became more established, teaching became the first profession that many women regularly pursued. However, in the early 19th century, education for women still mainly focused on improving their role in the home as wives and mothers.

Below: Paintings of the time, if not depicting women as wives and mothers, showed them lending a strong, maternal guiding hand—as in John J. Barralett's *America Guided by Wisdom*. In this painting, America is seated below the United States flag, with Minerva, the Roman goddess of wisdom, beside her. In front of the cottage at left are Ceres, the Roman goddess of agriculture, and Mercury, the god of commerce and travel. A statue of George Washington on a horse stands behind America and Minerva.

"A POOR PIECE OF FURNITURE"

"She has enough [intellect], and too much to make her exactly what I wish her to be. I mean only that her thurst [thirst] for reading, will probably obstruct the attainment of those amiable, condescending, and endearing manners, without which a woman is, in my estimation, but a poor piece of furniture."

Daniel Davis, a wealthy lawyer in Portland, Maine, writing about his teenage daughter in 1801

CHAPTER 7

DAILY LIFE

WOMEN STILL HAD MUCH TO DO IN THE HOME after the Revolution, and many, especially older women, stayed there and did not join the post-war workforce. The term "women's sphere" began to be used to describe women's different activities and duties both inside and outside the home.

TURNING POINT

BUYING AMERICAN GOODS

After the war, women's duties in support of the republic included denying themselves luxuries. In the fall of 1787, an anonymous author published "Address to the Ladies of America" in *American Museum*: "Your country is independent of European power: and your modes of dress should be independent of a group of coquettes [flirts], milliners [hat makers] and manufacturers, who, from motives of vanity on one hand, and avarice on the other, endeavour to enslave the fancy of the whole world." By buying items from the home market instead of more fashionable products from abroad, women supported American manufacturers.

Right: George Washington owned a plantation in Virginia and was wealthy. He is shown here with his family, all dressed in luxurious clothes.

RETREAT TO THE HOME

At the turn of the 19th century, women's work in the home generally included the care of as many as six or seven children. In the days before the invention of modern medicine eliminated most fatal childhood diseases, women had a large number of children because many of them were not expected to survive to adulthood. Wealthy families sometimes

Above: Many families remained poor after the Revolution. Government welfare programs did not exist, and so families had to make do as best they could. In this portrayal, a farm family enjoy one another's company and the children play with homemade toys.

hired tutors for the children. A typical middle-class family might consist of parents, children, a widowed aunt or sister (sometimes referred to horribly as the "relic"), and a few servants to help with the household chores and farming. An apprentice might live with the family to learn shoe making or another trade from the father.

In the South, slavery provided a source of free labor in the home. Southern plantation families, who lived far from neighbors, entertained many long-term guests. However, after 1808, slaves could no longer be imported from Africa into the United States. Because this limited the supply of slaves, slave owners were even more reluctant to let their workers buy their freedom. Slaves continued to struggle to keep their families together.

WOMEN OUTSIDE THE HOME

After the Revolution, middle-class women often had a choice about whether to work in the home, doing their traditional duties, or to teach school, to spend their days working in the family store, or, in the early 19th century, to work in the spinning mills. Poorer women in cities, especially recent immigrants, did

A HOUSE DIVIDED

"That women at present are by ignorance rendered vicious, is, I think, not to be disputed; and, that salutary effects tending to improve mankind might be expected from a REVOLUTION in female manners. . . . Justice and friendship are also set at defiance. . . . Children will never be properly educated till friendship subsists between parents. Virtue flies from a house divided against itself—and a whole legion of devils take up their residence there. . . . The affection of husbands and wives cannot be pure when they have so few sentiments in common, and when so little confidence is established at home, as must be the case when their pursuits are so different. That intimacy from which tenderness should flow, will not, cannot subsist between the vicious."

In *A Vindication on the Rights of Woman*, written in 1792, Mary Wollstonecraft describes the dangers that threaten family life when people, particularly women, are forced to remain ignorant.

Above: Frontier families often made long, hard journeys across the country to get to new land and a new life.

"

BRINGING UP CHILDREN

"I had much rather you should have found your Grave in the ocean you have crossd or any untimely death crop you in your Infant years rather than see you an immoral profligate [reckless person] or a Graceless child."

From a letter by Abigail Adams to her oldest son, John Quincy Adams, in 1778. Abigail was a strict mother who expected much of her three sons, John Quincy, Charles, and Thomas. She wanted them to be educated for public service and believed that after early childhood, boys should be taught only by men. Her strict parenting was successful in one instance— John Quincy became the sixth president of the United States—but her other two sons became alcoholics.

not always have the option of staying home and might work for a living as servants, nurses, seamstresses, or even prostitutes.

Frontier women had the exhausting and often frightening prospect of a long, dangerous journey to new lands. The women then had to summon their courage and endurance to settle the lands once they arrived there. After the Louisiana Purchase in 1803, families flocked west, migrating to remote places such as Detroit, Michigan, a frontier outpost.

Native Americans still mostly lived outside the towns and cities of the United States. Before the Revolution, farming had been the women's responsibility, but after the war, men in Native American families turned from hunting to farming. Women adapted to living alongside the settlers, learning skills such as how to weave cloth and churn butter, but they lost much of the political power they had enjoyed in their tribes.

SYMBOLS OF VIRTUE

In the early 19th century, women who stayed home were increasingly isolated there while the men went out to work. Women began to be seen as creating a safe haven for men from the busy outside world with its stresses, competition, and low morals. Women had always been considered the better-behaved sex, but now they were elevated to a symbol of virtue, sacrificing themselves for their families. In the new country, women also had the vital role of raising young citizens who would preserve the republic.

INCREASED LITERACY

Improved schooling meant that many more women were literate in the early 19th century. Another reason they were better informed was that their political awareness had been raised during the war. They were better able to educate their young children, including their

BREAKTHROUGH BIOGRAPHY

JUDITH SARGENT MURRAY (1751–1820)

Writing under the pseudonym Constantia, Judith Sargent Murray published an essay column called "The Gleaner" in the *Massachusetts Magazine* in the early 1790s. In her essays, she stressed the importance of self-confidence in girls so that they could prepare for an independent future. "Marriage should not be presented as [women's] *sumum bonum* [highest achievement], or as a certain, or even necessary event; they should learn to respect a single life, and even regard it as the most *eligible*, except a warm, mutual and judicious attachment had gained the ascendancy in the bosom," she wrote. She went on to say that young women should be "qualified to administer by their *own efforts to their own wants*" and "independence should be placed within their grasp." A three-volume collection of Murray's "Gleaner" essays was published in 1798. George Washington and John Adams were among those who bought copies of her book.

Left: Judith Sargent Murray was a thoughtful and perceptive essayist who speculated in her writings about women's possibilities in the republic.

daughters, and wanted to send their children to good schools. The expectations of schooling were still different for daughters, however. The textbook *American Preceptor* stated: "Our young men will be emulous [eager] to exceed the geniuses of the east; our daughters will shine as bright constellations in the sphere where nature placed them."

Educated, politically aware women expected to be companions with their husbands, not duty-bound wives. "Mutual esteem, mutual friendship, mutual confidence, *begirt about by mutual forbearance* [patient self-control]" are the requirements for a successful marriage," wrote essayist Judith Sargent Murray in 1784.

RELIGION

Before the Revolutionary War, ministers in churches often reminded women in their sermons that they were the descendants of Eve in the Bible, who was tempted to sin by the serpent in the Garden of Eden. More women than men attended church. Women might have done more soul searching than men in those days since they faced the

Below: Church was a very important spiritual and social part of American life both before and after the Revolution.

AN ENCHANTING REPOSE

"It is at home, where man . . . seeks a refuge from the vexations and embarrassments of business, an enchanting repose from exertion, a relaxation from care by the interchange of affection: where some of his finest sympathies, tastes, and moral and religious feelings are formed and nourished;—where is the treasury of pure disinterested love, such as is seldom found in the busy walks of a selfish and calculating world."

In 1827, a New Hampshire pastor has high expectations of the home life a woman should provide.

Above: Dolley Madison stayed in the president's house to retrieve valuables despite warnings that the British were coming.

WOMEN OF COURAGE AND CONVICTION

DOLLEY MADISON (1768–1849)

Dolley Madison was widowed at age twenty-five, then married James Madison, who would become the fourth president of the United States. A gracious hostess and warmhearted friend, as first lady Dolley was famous for her dinner parties and receptions. During the War of 1812 (America's second war with the British), Dolley bravely stayed behind at the president's mansion as British troops attacked Washington. She packed important state papers, the official Gilbert Stuart portrait of George Washington, and other valuables, saving them from the British, who burned the mansion down. (The new house built for the president was painted white and became known as the White House.) "I have always been an advocate for fighting when assailed," Dolley said. After James Madison's death, Dolley struggled with poverty but retained her kind, lively spirit. At age eighty, she helped to raise funds to build the Washington Monument.

possibility of early death in childbirth and often the heartbreaking, unexplained deaths of their children.

The French Revolution in 1789 promoted atheism and at first resulted in anarchy in France. Its influence was felt throughout Europe and across the Atlantic. Ministers of churches and their congregations in the United States organized to fight atheism and anarchy through the Protestant religion. This time of religious revival, called the Second Great Awakening, lasted from about the 1790s to the 1840s. Wanting to involve women, ministers referred less often in their sermons to Eve and spoke more about the many heroines in the Bible. The ministers also advised that mothers were the best people to teach religion to their children.

Above: The temperance movement began in response to the often terrible effects of alcoholism on families.

TURNING POINT

THE AMERICAN SOCIETY FOR THE PROMOTION OF TEMPERANCE

In 1826, ministers of churches formed the American Society for the Promotion of Temperance to try to end the drinking of liquor in the United States. To involve as many people as possible, the new society distributed newspapers and other printed materials and sent organizers to communities across the country. By 1835, more than 1.5 million people belonged to the society—20 percent of the population. Many women joined the society since they often experienced financial ruin and abuse if the income earner of the family drank too much. Women were also regarded as the family's moral center. The American Society for the Promotion of Temperance was another gathering that honed women's organizational and business skills.

Christianity provided women with proof that they were equal to men in God's eyes: according to Christian teachings, women and men both had immortal souls and the same moral conduct was expected of both. In 1810, Joseph Buckminster, a minister in Boston, said in a sermon that Christianity made "men willing to treat females as equals, and in some respects, as superiors." But Buckminster also felt women should pay for this honor by giving service to the Christian religion to support and spread it. Missionaries in foreign lands said that only Christianity supported this kind of equality of women with men.

RELIGIOUS SOCIETIES

Aware of their important new role as agents of religious instruction, women organized their own religious societies at church. Sewing circles raised money for charity, and other church-based societies advocated temperance, helped orphans, and engaged in other activities to help the poor. The many women working in factories in the early 18th century were required by the mill owners to attend church. This gave them the opportunity to form church-based societies. Southern women, often isolated on plantations or farms, formed fewer organizations, and poor women living on farms had no time for them. Although the societies centered on traditional causes, through them women learned how to run meetings, speak in public, and raise money.

Starting in about 1820, ministers' sermons about women again turned restrictive, an alarmed reaction to changing social patterns, such as more women in the workforce. In his sermon to the New York Female Missionary Society in 1825, titled "The Excellence and Influence of the Female Character," Minister Gardiner Spring stated: "There are spheres for which a female is not fitted, and from which the God of nature has proscribed [banned] her." But in many ways women already had the experience and skills to leave the sphere of domesticity for those spheres deemed unsuitable by Minister Spring, such as the workplace and politics. In the coming decades, women's work in the antislavery and women's suffrage movements grew out of their experience in church-based societies.

WOMEN OF COURAGE AND CONVICTION

SACAJAWEA (c. 1786–1812)

Sacajawea was a Native American of the Shoshone tribe who served as an interpreter on the exploratory expedition of Meriwether Lewis and William Clark to the Pacific Ocean. The expedition had been charged by Thomas Jefferson, then the president of the United States, to explore the lands of the Louisiana Purchase, bought by the United States from France on May 2, 1803. The acquisition of these lands had more than doubled the size of the United States. The expedition was also required to search for a northwest passage to the Pacific. Sacajawea and her husband, Toussaint Charbonneau, were hired in what is now North Dakota to translate the languages of Native Americans whom the expedition might meet along the way. Sacajawea played a vital role in guiding the group, negotiating the purchase of horses from Native Americans and persuading them that her group had peaceful intentions.

Left: Sacajawea helped lead the expedition of Lewis and Clark to the Pacific Ocean.

THE PERIOD IN BRIEF

THE DAUGHTERS OF LIBERTY SOCIETIES, FORMED BY WOMEN JUST before the Revolutionary War, were the first real involvement of colonial women in politics. In the chaos of the Revolution and the freedom it afforded, women formed more societies, such as the Ladies' Association of Philadelphia, to help win the war. Women's brave and unusual activities during the war as soldiers, spies, and businesspeople set a precedent for women's leadership roles in the mid-19th century.

Above: Elizabeth Cady Stanton built on her experiences at the Troy Female Seminary to organize the movement for women's right to vote.

NEW DEVELOPMENTS

In the new United States, women's magazines had examined women's roles in marriage, child rearing, and preserving the republic. Women had undertaken new and unexpected quests, such as Sacajawea's daring journey with explorers Lewis and Clark. Women's academies and seminaries flourished, teaching not only the traditionally feminine subjects such as music and painting but those formerly reserved almost entirely for men, such as mathematics and philosophy. Famous graduates of Emma Willard's Troy Female Seminary included Elizabeth Cady Stanton, who started the first organized women's rights and women's suffrage movements in the United States. By 1840, literacy was almost universal among New Englanders, both men and women.

AFRICAN AMERICANS AND NATIVE AMERICANS

African-American women remained trapped in slavery before and after the Revolution. True freedom for black men and women would have to wait for the American Civil War and beyond. Native American women lost status and power as a result of the war as settlers took over more and more Native American territory. Native Americans lost much of their heritage and traditional ways of life during this period.

WORK AND ASSOCIATIONS

In the early 1800s, the rise of industrialization in the United States resulted in many women working outside the home, especially in textile factories. At first, women's wages were low and working conditions hard, but soon women had organized to improve their work life. The first women's strike at the Dover textile factory in 1828 was unsuccessful, but the stage was set for more effective strikes soon to come later in the 19th century.

Although many women were leaving the home, a movement had begun for them to return there, keeping to their "sphere" as a way of producing virtuous citizens and preserving the new country. Nevertheless, women found new independence, forming religious associations, including prayer groups, charitable associations, and missionary and education societies, and assuming positions of leadership. As the 1820s drew to a close, women leaders in business, education, and religion were poised for the struggle to win the most important of women's rights—the vote.

Right: Women served in the American Revolution as both soldiers in battle and on the homefront. Afterward, as dedicated patriots, they became symbolic soldiers, preserving the country's republican values by raising the next generations of Americans and increasingly involving themselves in civic life.

PROPER EDUCATION OF CHILDREN

"There is no subject concerning which I feel more anxiety than the proper education of my children. . . . Governors & kings have only to enact laws & compel men to observe them—mothers have to implant ideas and cultivate dispositions which can alone make good citizens or subjects— . . . the mother's task is to mould the infant's character into whatever shape she pleases."

From the diary of Susan Huntington, 1813

Timeline

1765   March 22: The Stamp Act is passed by the British Parliament to pay for the costs of administering the British colonies.

1767   June 27: The Townsend Act forces the American colonies to pay taxes on glass, paint, oil, lead, paper, and tea. American women organize to produce homemade replacements. Often these groups call themselves the Daughters of Liberty.

1768   August 1: Merchants and traders in Boston sign the Boston Non-Importation Agreement.

1770   March 5: The Boston Massacre, a riot, begins when about fifty people attack a British sentinel. The British soldiers open fire, killing four people.

1773   May 10: The Tea Act is passed by the British Parliament.
December 16: The Boston Tea Party.

1774   March–June: The British Parliament passes five laws that the colonists call the Intolerable Acts.
September 5–October 26: The Continental Congress, a group of delegates from each of the thirteen colonies, gathers in Philadelphia to discuss the colonists' grievances.
October 25: Fifty-one women in Edenton, North Carolina, sign the Edenton Resolution, vowing to abstain from tea, cloth, and other luxuries imported from England.

1775   April 19: The American Revolution starts.
May 10: The Second Continental Congress meets in Philadelphia. The delegates agree to create an army to fight the British and to print money to pay for it. In late May, Betsy Ross is chosen to sew the first American flag.
May: Mary Goddard is listed on the masthead of the *Maryland Journal* as editor and publisher. Benjamin Franklin appoints her as postmaster.

1776   July 4: Congress adopts the Declaration of Independence, in which the colonies declare their independence from British rule.
September 15: The British occupy New York City.
November 16: During the battle of Fort Washington in New York, Margaret Corbin takes over her husband's cannon and is wounded.

1777   September 26: The British occupy Philadelphia.

1778   June 18: The British abandon Philadelphia.
June 28: Washington's army forces the British to retreat at Monmouth Courthouse, New Jersey.

1779   Samuel Slater introduces industrial spinning machinery to New England.

1780   May 12: Charleston, South Carolina, falls to British forces.
June 10: Esther De Berdt Reed writes "The Sentiments of an American Woman," published in the *Pennsylvania Gazette*, outlining a plan to mobilize all American women to collect money for the soldiers. Her organization becomes known as the Ladies' Association of Philadelphia, and similar organizations

quickly spread to other towns.
July 11: French troops arrive in Newport, Rhode Island, to aide the Americans.

1781	October 19: General Charles Cornwallis surrenders to the Americans and French at Yorktown, Virginia.
1783	September 3: The United States and Britain sign the Treaty of Paris, in Paris, France, ending the Revolutionary War. November 25: British troops leave New York City.
1787	September 17: The United States Constitution is signed.
1789	April 30: George Washington becomes the first president of the United States. Martha Washington becomes first lady. July 14: Insurgents in France storm the Bastille, a prison seen to be a symbol of royal tyranny. On August 26, the National Constituent Assembly publishes the Declaration of the Rights of Man and the Citizen, modeled on the United States' Declaration of Independence.
1790	Judith Sargent Murray publishes in the *Massachusetts Magazine* her essay "On the Equality of the Sexes." December 20: Samuel Slater builds a water-powered cotton mill in Pawtucket, Rhode Island. It makes possible the move from home manufacture to factory production of textiles.
1792	Mary Wollstonecraft publishes *Vindication on the Rights of Women*.
1797	March 4: John Adams is sworn in as the second president of the United States. Abigail Adams is first lady.
1798	Murray publishes *The Gleaner*, a three-volume book of essays and plays.
1801	March 4: Thomas Jefferson becomes the

third president of the United States. A widower, Jefferson has no first lady.

1803	May 2: The United States completes the Louisiana Purchase with France, buying 828,000 square miles of new territory west of the thirteen original colonies. A few weeks later, President Thomas Jefferson gets $2,500 from Congress to fund the Lewis and Clark expedition to explore the territory.
1804	May 18: The French Senate proclaims Napoleon Bonaparte emperor.
1805	April: Sacajawea, of the Shoshone tribe, helps guide explorers Meriwether Lewis and William Clark from Missouri to the Pacific Ocean. November 18: The Lewis and Clark expedition reaches the Pacific Ocean.
1809	March 4: James Madison becomes the fourth president of the United States.
1812–14	The United States wins a second war against Britain.
1815	June 18: Napoleon is defeated at Waterloo by the British and Prussians.
1817	March 4: James Monroe becomes the fifth president of the United States.
1821	September: Emma Willard opens the Troy Female Seminary, the first publicly funded school for women.
1824	In the Pawtucket, Rhode Island, textile mills, 102 female textile workers join a strike with their male coworkers, protesting wage cuts and increased work hours. This is the first time women workers have joined a strike.
1825	March 4: John Quincy Adams, son of John and Abigail Adams, becomes the sixth president of the United States.
1828	In Dover, New Hampshire, women go on strike at a mill. They return to work before the strike is settled.

GLOSSARY AND FURTHER INFORMATION

atheism The belief that no god exists.

blacklist To be put on a list of people not to be given a job.

boycott To refuse to deal with someone such as a store or organization to show disapproval and attempt to achieve change.

card An instrument or machine for carding fibers that usually consists of bent wire teeth set closely in rows in a thick piece of leather fastened to a back.

carding Cleaning, disentangling, and collecting fibers by the use of cards, preparatory to spinning.

colonist Someone who settles in a new country.

colony A group of people living in a new territory but retaining ties with the parent state.

common law The unwritten law developed in England mostly from judicial decisions based on custom and precedent that constitutes the basis of the English and United States legal system.

composition A school exercise in the form of a brief essay.

constitution The basic principles and laws of a nation, state, or social group that determine the powers and duties of the government and guarantee certain rights to the people in it.

Continental Army The official army of the thirteen original colonies that became the United States, established by a resolution of the Continental Congress on May 10, 1775.

Continental Congress A convention of delegates from the thirteen colonies that became the governing body of the United States during the Revolution. The Continental Congress met from 1774 to 1789 and was replaced with the United States Congress.

cottage industry A business in which the workers are a family or individuals working at home with their own equipment.

dry goods Products such as textiles, and ready-to-wear clothing.

effigy A crude representation, usually of a hated person.

English common law Law developed over many centuries in England, based on common sense and previous law cases that had come before judges.

founding father A leading person in the founding of the United States; specifically, a member of the American Constitutional Convention of 1787.

immigrant A person who moves to another country to live.

Industrial Revolution Usually refers to late-18th-century England; a rapid change to use of power-driven machinery or an important change in the types or uses of such machinery.

inoculate To introduce something into the human body, such as a virus, to prevent a disease.

loyalist An American colonist who remained loyal to Britain at the time of the Revolutionary War.

masthead The part of a newspaper or magazine that lists the title of the publication, the positions of the staff, and details about the publication's ownership, advertising, and subscription rates.

militia A group of citizens organized for military service.

missionary A person who spreads his or her faith.

moral Conforming to a standard of correct behavior.

New England The northeast part of the United States, including the states of Connecticut, Maine, Massachusetts, New Hampshire, Vermont, and Rhode Island.

piecework Work paid at a set price per piece.

prohibit Forbid.

Puritan A member of a 16th- and 17th-century Protestant group in England and New England that opposed as unscriptural, or not according to the Bible, the ceremonies of worship and the church government of the Church of England, England's official church.

Quaker A Christian group that opposes war and ordained ministers (ministers given authority over other church members).

quarter Give lodging to.

ratify To approve or confirm formally.

redcoat A British soldier, especially in the Revolutionary War. Most British soldiers wore red coats as part of their uniform.

republic A government in which supreme power resides in a body of citizens entitled to vote and is exercised by elected officials and representatives responsible to them and governing according to law.

rhetoric The study of writing or speaking as a means of communication or persuasion.

Roman law The codification, or summarizing and writing down, of law in Rome, first done in 450 B.C.E.; sometimes called civil law. A legal system derived from Roman law has legislation as its foundation.

smallpox A contagious disease caused by a virus that resulted in skin sores. Smallpox vaccines now prevent smallpox worldwide, but in the 18th and 19th centuries, the disease was often disfiguring or fatal.

suffrage The right to vote.

tar and feather To coat a person with hot tar and feathers as an insult and punishment.

temperance Moderation or abstinence from the use of alcoholic beverages.

yarn A continuous strand or strands made of either natural or man-made fibers and used in weaving and knitting to form cloth.

BOOKS

Bryan, Helen. *Martha Washington: First Lady of Liberty*. New York: Wiley, 2002.

Cott, Nancy F. *The Bonds of Womanhood: "Woman's Sphere" in New England, 1780–1835*. New Haven: Yale University Press, 1977.

Kerber, Linda K. *Women of the Republic: Intellect and Ideology in Revolutionary America*. Chapel Hill: University of North Carolina Press, 1980.

Mattern, David B., and Holly C. Shulman, eds. *The Selected Letters of Dolley Payne Madison*. Charlottesville, Virginia: University of Virginia Press, 2003.

Norton, Mary Beth. *Liberty's Daughters: The Revolutionary Experience of American Women, 1750–1800*. Ithaca, New York: Cornell University Press, 1980.

Roberts, Cokie. *Founding Mothers: The Women Who Shaped Our Nation*. New York: Harper, 2005.

Roberts, Cokie. *Ladies of Liberty: The Women Who Shaped Our Nation*. New York: Morrow, 2008.

Sedgwick, Catharine. 1827. *Hope Leslie, Or, Early Times in the Massachusetts*. 1827. London: Penguin, 2009.

Sedgwick, Catharine. 1822. *A New-England Tale: Or, Sketches of New-England Character and Manners*. New York: Oxford University Press, 2003.

Shuffelton, Frank. *The Letters of John and Abigail Adams*. London: Penguin, 2004.

Wollstonecraft, Mary. *Mary, a Fiction*, and *Maria: or, the Wrongs of Woman*. 1778, 1798. London: Penguin, 2004.

Wollstonecraft, Mary. *A Vindication of the Rights of Woman*. 1792. London: Penguin, 2004.

WEB SITES

http://www.colonialancestors.com/revolutionary/women.htm

http://www.georgiaencyclopedia.org/

http://www.ushistory.org/

http://www.earlyamerica.com

http://www.msa.md.gov/

INDEX